Collins
INTERNATIONAL

Science
Foundation Plus
Activity Book B

Published by Collins
An imprint of HarperCollins*Publishers*
The News Building, 1 London Bridge Street,
London, SE1 9GF, UK

HarperCollins*Publishers*
Macken House, 39/40 Mayor Street Upper,
Dublin 1, D01 C9W8, Ireland

Browse the complete Collins catalogue at
www.collins.co.uk

© HarperCollins*Publishers* Limited 2021

10 9 8 7 6 5 4

ISBN 978-0-00-846874-3

British Library Cataloguing-in-Publication Data
A catalogue record for this publication is available from the British Library.

Author: Fiona Macgregor
Publisher: Elaine Higgleton
Product manager: Letitia Luff
Commissioning editor: Rachel Houghton
Researcher: Andi Colombo
Edited by: Eleanor Barber
Editorial management: Oriel Square
Cover designer: Kevin Robbins
Cover illustrations: Jouve India Pvt Ltd.
Internal illustrations: Jouve India Pvt. Ltd.; p 8–9 Tasneem Amiruddin
Typesetter: Jouve India Pvt. Ltd.
Production controller: Lyndsey Rogers
Printed and bound in India by
Replika Press Pvt. Ltd.

Acknowledgements

With thanks to all the kindergarten staff and their schools around the world who
have helped with the development of this course, by sharing insights and
commenting on and testing sample materials:

Calcutta International School: Sharmila Majumdar, Mrs Pratima Nayar, Preeti
Roychoudhury, Tinku Yadav, Lakshmi Khanna, Mousumi Guha, Radhika Dhanuka,
Archana Tiwari, Urmita Das; Gateway College (Sri Lanka): Kousala Benedict; Hawar
International School: Kareen Barakat, Shahla Mohammed, Jennah Hussain; Manthan
International School: Shalini Reddy; Monterey Pre-Primary: Adina Oram; Prometheus
School: Aneesha Sahni, Deepa Nanda; Pragyanam School: Monika Sachdev; Rosary
Sisters High School: Samar Sabat, Sireen Freij, Hiba Mousa; Solitaire Global School:
Devi Nimmagadda; United Charter Schools (UCS): Tabassum Murtaza; Vietnam
Australia International School: Holly Simpson

The publishers wish to thank the following for permission to reproduce photographs.

(t = top, c = centre, b = bottom, r = right, l = left)

p 14tl Eric Isselee/Shutterstock, p 14tr Boonrod/Shutterstock, p 14cl1 Irina
Maksimova/Shutterstock, p 14cr1 Paul Cotney/Shutterstock, p 14cl2 Ilya Zlotnikov/
Shutterstock, p 14cr2 Nynke van Holten/Shutterstock, p 14bl Dora Zett/Shutterstock,
p 14br Eric Isselee/Shutterstock, p 22t Volodymyr Goinyk/Shutterstock, p 22c1
nektofadeev/Shutterstock, p 22c2 Fer Gregory/Shutterstock, p 22b muratart/
Shutterstock

MIX
Paper | Supporting
responsible forestry
FSC™ C007454

FSC
www.fsc.org

This book is produced from independently certified FSC™
paper to ensure responsible forest management.

For more information visit:
www.harpercollins.co.uk/green

Match

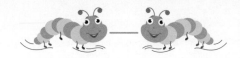

The sun gives us ...

light

heat

food

Match the word to the picture.

Date:

Match

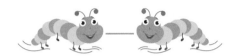

Animals need ...

PCM 9. Cut out the words.
Stick them in the correct place.   Date:

Circle and say

Circle the things a cat needs. Say what they are.

Date:

Draw

1

2

1 Draw the seeds that were kept in the cupboard.
2 Draw the seeds that were kept in a sunny place.
Say what is different about them.   Date:

Match

underwater

forest

desert

Match the plant to its habitat.

Date:

Follow

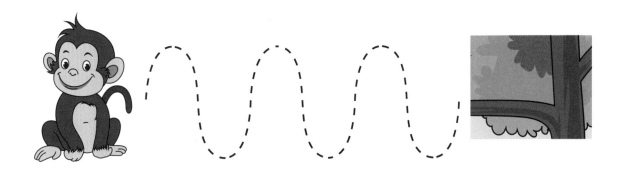

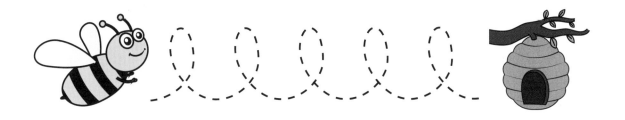

Trace the lines to help the animals get to their homes.

Date:

Cut and stick

PCM 12. Cut out the animals.
Stick them in their habitats.

Date:

Circle and match

Find the animals in their homes in the big picture.
Draw lines to the big picture.

Date:

Cut and stick

PCM 13. Cut out the pictures.
Stick them in the correct place.

Date:

Sort

Solid	Liquid

PCM 14. Cut out the pictures.
Stick them in the correct box.

Date:

Try this

My object	Does it float (✓) or sink (✗)?
stone	
metal teaspoon	
plastic teaspoon	
pencil	

Test some objects to see if they float or sink.
Put a ✓ if they float. Put a ✗ if they sink.

Date:

Follow

Help the water droplet find the plant roots.

Date:

Match and say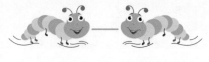

goat

horse

elephant

dog

calf

puppy

kid

foal

Draw lines to match the adult and young animals.
Name them.   Date:

Cut and stick

Chickens lay

⬜ ⬜.

⬜  hatch out of

the eggs.

A chick grows into an adult

⬜ 🐔.

The chicken lays ⬜ ⬜ ⬜.

PCM 15. Cut out the words. Stick them in the correct place to finish the sentences. Use the pictures to help you. Date:

Draw

caterpillar

eggs

chrysalis

butterfly

Draw the missing butterfly.	
Date:	

Cut and stick

PCM 16. Cut out the pictures and stick them in the correct place.

Date:

Circle and say

Look at the pictures. What is different? What is the same? Circle the things that are different.   Date:

Draw

1

2

1 Draw the sky in the morning.
2 Draw the sky at night.   Date:

Find and colour

sun

tree

fire

torch

moon

stars

lamp

candle

light

Colour the things that gives us light at night.

Date:

Find and colour

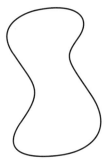
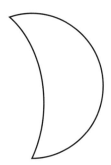

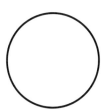

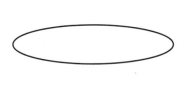

Colour in the moon shapes.

Date:

Match

The sun gives light and heat.

Animals need food.

Does it float?

Some plants grow underwater.

Match the sentences to the pictures.

Date:

Tick

☐ I can match.

☐ I can circle.

☐ I can draw.

☐ I can follow.

☐ I can cut and stick.

☐ I can sort.

☐ I can try things.

☐ I can find and colour.

Tick what you can do.

Date:

Assessment record

_____ has achieved these Science Foundation Plus Phase Objectives:

Know that a plant needs water and sunlight to grow and stay alive	1	2	3
Identify some needs of animals: air, water, food, shelter	1	2	3
Know that plants grow best in certain habitats	1	2	3
Know that some animals live underground	1	2	3
Explore how heating and cooling lead to changes in everyday familiar materials (melting, solidifying)	1	2	3
Classify other objects as liquid or solid	1	2	3
Describe objects in terms of whether they sink or float	1	2	3
Recognise that living things change as they grow	1	2	3
Know that the sun gives us light	1	2	3
Identify the main observable differences between the sky at night and during the day	1	2	3
Observe that when we look at the moon over time, it appears to change shape	1	2	3

1: Partially achieved
2: Achieved
3: Exceeded

Signed by teacher:
Signed by parent:

Date: